# let's celebrate a
# baptism

GW00692248

## CONTENTS

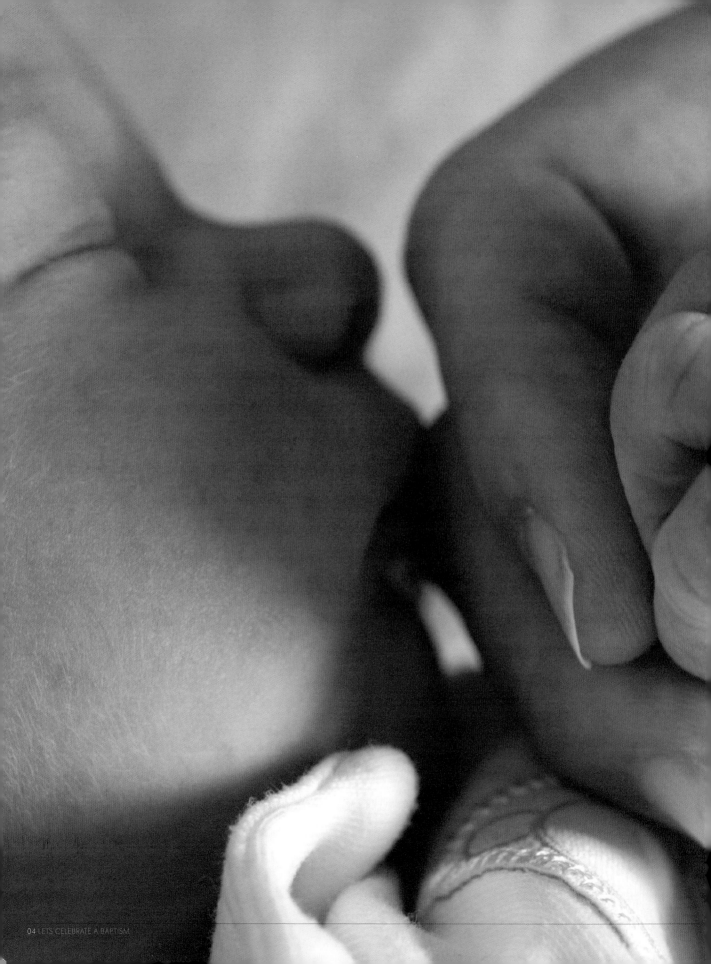

# congratulations

Every parent wants the best for their child. The birth of a baby causes us to pause and reflect on what we hope for this new life entrusted to us. For Christians, this hope is expressed in baptism and the invitation it offers their child to share in the life and Spirit of God. God also wants the best for every one of us and this desire is shown in the life and words of Jesus Christ. Traditionally, for Christians, the arrival of a new baby means a baptism.

**BAPTISM OFFERS:**
- the public naming of your child for all to hear
- parents the opportunity to make a public commitment to the care and well-being of their child
- the recognition of chosen adults as godparents and/or witnesses
- friends, family and the wider community a chance to welcome the new arrival and voice their support for the family

At the heart of baptism, though, is the initiation into the Christian community – the Church. To be baptised is to become a Christian and experience, for life, both the blessings and the responsibilities of that commitment. As a parent, you'll make promises on behalf of your child. We'd like to help you prepare for this sacred celebration and for the days that follow. Our parish wants to welcome you and your child in the way that you feel is most appropriate. If, having read this booklet, you the parents would prefer more time and reflection before making the commitment to full Christian membership on behalf of your child, please let your parish priest know. It may be possible to offer you a simple blessing service for your baby if you prefer at this stage.

# getting started

There's a few things you should think about before arranging a baptism...

■ Your priest or a member of the baptism team, will explain to you the ways in which our parish welcomes a new Christian. Don't be shy about mentioning any issues that concern you, or any particular aspects of the ceremony which you find confusing.

■ Check what dates are available before you make any other plans.

■ Think about your choice of godparents. Godparents should be committed Catholics who are at least sixteen years of age and be baptised and confirmed.

■ If there's someone who is important to you or your partner who isn't a Catholic but who you'd want to play a significant part in your child's life, why not invite that person to be an official witness at the baptism?

■ If you, the parents, are from different faith backgrounds make sure that you take time to talk about this as soon as possible. How will you develop a united approach to the faith development of your child while also respecting your own different religious experiences?

■ Are you sure that baptism for your child is what you really want? Parents can be placed under considerable pressure from others to ask for baptism for their baby, even though they might not be comfortable with that decision. If this is happening to you please talk about it to the parish priest who will understand your situation and will want to help you make the right decision for you and your baby.

"As your child grows, may your love and commitment cherish what begins at baptism, so that your child will always have the courage and the confidence to follow the Gospel of Jesus Christ throughout life."

## Checklist

✓ Confirm dates for baptism preparation
✓ Confirm date for baptism
✓ Think about possible scripture readings
✓ Choose godparents
✓ Choose witnesses if appropriate
✓ Prepare prayers of intercession
✓ Plan your family celebration

# celebrating
# anewcreation

## We feel instinctively the mystery of creation

The creation of your child is a sign of life: God's life moving within you, your love and your relationship. It's also a sign of hope for the future. This miracle of life is all around us in many different ways and it's within these signs that we see and experience the presence of God.

### THE TOUCH OF GOD

We feel instinctively the mystery of creation — the mystery of love — in ways we're often unable to express in words. The touch of a hand, a fleeting glance, or a certain smile between people in love, can speak more eloquently than any words. Equally, a solitary tear can reveal unspeakable pain or sadness. This variety of signs of life and love help us to sense the touch of the Creator in our world. But God doesn't play hide and seek. He sent us his Son, Jesus Christ to show us his love in a totally real way.

Jesus reached out to people wherever they were and whatever situation they were living in. He offered a fresh beginning to all who chose to accept his words. Jesus changed lives. He was put to death on the cross but rose to new life, witnessed by many. The sign of his resurrection was the foundation of the Christian community — the Church; the living sign of Christ's presence in the world today.

## A sacrament of life

As Christians, our unity with Christ is maintained and strengthened at special moments during which we draw especially close to Christ by recalling his life and actions. We call these special events sacraments.

At these times we experience the love of God through ordinary human experiences: being born into a family, sharing a meal, being healed, forgiven. Just as the shared glance between lovers is a sign of total unity, so the signs we use as Christians illustrate our union with God, which words cannot describe.

A sacrament is a sign of life — God's life, eternal life. Baptism is for your child the gateway to all other sacraments.

### WHAT ARE THE 7 CHRISTIAN SACRAMENTS?

- Baptism
- Confirmation
- Eucharist

These are the signs that we have become Christians. They are called the Sacraments of Initiation. Baptism and Confirmation are signs of our birth as Christians and so can never be repeated.

- Marriage
- Holy Orders

These are signs that we want to make a sincere commitment to loving and serving God and others.

- Reconciliation
- Anointing

During our lives we fall sick either physically, mentally or spiritually. We need healing and a chance to begin again. These are the signs through which we experience God's continuing healing love and forgiveness towards us, both throughout life and as we face death.

# the story of baptism:

**1**

*Gospel of Jesus Christ*

John the Baptist

River Jordan

**2**

*700 AD*

*Eastertime (Passover)*

Catechumens

## Stage 1 The New Testament

John the Baptist offered baptism as a sign of repentance and change. John's baptism of Jesus confirmed that Jesus was in fact God made man; that he was truly human in our world.

At his own Ascension, Jesus told his apostles, "Make disciples of all the nations, baptise them in the name of the Father and of the Son and of the Holy Spirit." This is the heart of Christian baptism — conversion to a life of faith and its demands of a different lifestyle with different priorities.

In the very first days of the Church, baptism involved adults taking a period of preparation sometimes lasting up to three years. Those who asked to be baptised were called 'catechumens' which means 'under instruction'. At the celebration of the baptism the person was submerged in the water (often a flowing river) as a sign of being "buried with Christ" (St Paul Romans 6:4) The newly baptised person then rose from the water as a sign of the resurrection of Christ — which they, too, now shared.

## Stage 2 Throughout history

As Christianity spread, whole households were received into the Church, and Christian parents increasingly sought baptism for their children. By the year 700AD the majority of baptisms were of infants. As a result the extended period of preparation was no longer undertaken. Baptisms were usually celebrated at Eastertime.

Traditionally, in the Early Church, the bishop was central to the ceremony as it was the bishop who sealed the baptised with oil of chrism and the laying on of hands. However, the increasing numbers resulted in parish priests celebrating baptisms in the absence of the bishop. At a later date, those who had been baptised would be brought to the bishop for the 'laying on of hands' at which he confirmed the earlier celebration performed by the priest.

The reception of Holy Communion followed at a later date. Here we see the origin of the three sacraments of Christian initiation: Baptism, Confirmation and Holy Communion (or Eucharist).

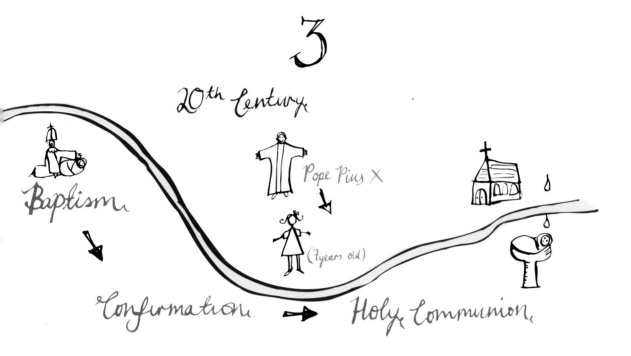

*3*

20th Century

Baptism

Pope Pius X

(7 years old)

Confirmation → Holy Communion

## Stage 3 Modern times

In time, the Church declared that only those who had 'reached the age of reason' — about seven years old — could receive the Sacrament of Confirmation. This marked the full separation of baptism and confirmation. Later teaching preferred that only candidates over 12 years of age should receive confirmation, "in order to strengthen their resolve".

By the beginning of the 20th century many people attended church regularly but few received Holy Communion. Pope Pius X was concerned at this and lowered the age for first receiving Holy Communion to seven years old. As a result the rites of initiation as a Christian — Baptism, Confirmation and Holy Communion, became further fragmented and can sometimes seem to be unrelated events.

Today, the Church is reclaiming the tradition and the sacred connections between all three sacraments, which unite us in the family of Jesus Christ.

In recent years, the Christian community, the Church, has reflected upon the true nature of baptism and its role. In baptism your child becomes a full member of the Christian family. Your child shares in the blessing and consecration of the oils, and shares in the life of Jesus Christ. This is the sacred tradition which your child becomes part of, from the day of his or her baptism.

# friends and family
## ... preparing a celebration for all

### OLDER FRIENDS AND RELATIVES

■ Why not invite senior members of the family and/or long-standing friends to read or recite one of the prayers at the baptism.

■ A wonderful gift from this generation is a scrapbook or written record of your own baptism, or other family religious ceremonies, to illustrate your family traditions.

■ Alternatively, perhaps they could compile a simple photo album featuring earlier generations?

■ You'll need a white garment for the ceremony (usually a shawl). Is there one in the family which could be used, or would someone make one for this happy event?

■ Ask older relatives if there are any deceased members of the family who they'd like remembered in the prayers on the day.

### OTHER CHILDREN

■ Don't be shy about inviting other children to the baptism. Baptism should be seen as a community event.

■ You could ask them to make some pictures to decorate the church with.

■ How about asking them to make a baptism book for your baby which will be a memento for when your child grows up? You could offer to supply some photos to complete it after the event.

■ Ask older children to compose some simple prayers to read at the ceremony.

■ Do you have any teenagers who could welcome people as they arrive and hand out booklets or guides to the service.

### FAMILY AND FRIENDS WHO ARE NOT CATHOLIC

■ There will probably be a number of family and friends who are not Catholics present at your child's baptism. By planning ahead you can ensure that everyone present feels part of the celebration whilst not being put in any situation which might make them feel uncomfortable.

■ By providing a simple outline to the ceremony including its purpose and symbolism, you can help people feel at home (see template on page 29).

■ In many families with a variety of religious traditions it's the custom to ask a close relative or special friend to be a witness to the baptism and to play a special role in the future life of the child.

### CHOOSING A GODPARENT

Godparents were originally chosen as supporters to the baptised in a time when many people were being baptised as adults and didn't have the Christian family support we have now. Today, godparents continue to fulfil an important role both as guides and mentors. To be an authentic support, a godparent must have some understanding of their role and of the faith. For this reason, the Church asks that godparents be at least 16 years old, and to have been baptised and confirmed themselves.

When preparing for baptism, don't forget to consider ways in which to involve those closest to you. Family and belonging are at the heart of baptism. It's all about becoming a member of the family of the Christian community as well as celebrating your family faith tradition. Try to ensure that the celebrations reflect this theme. By involving others — and that includes your close friends, your 'extended family' — you'll be re-creating your child's family in a fresh way.

Godparents
fulfill an
important
role both as
guides and
mentors

## After the church service

A simple celebration is all that people expect when you have a new baby. Don't allow yourself to be steamrollered into anything which is too costly or which is not of your own choice. Remember, this is your child's baptism and as a parent you can make the decisions.

# questions
## you may have...

**Q** I'd like to choose an original name for my little boy. Are there any restrictions on my choice?

**A** Traditionally, Christians chose the names of saints for their children. It was the custom to choose a patron saint who would be a spiritual guardian for the child throughout life. Today, many Christians retain that custom but there are often other traditions which are also important within families. It may be that you or your partner's family have a particular name which is important to you. There may be a special person who has died whom you want to remember by giving their name to your child.

Choose a name (or names) for your little boy which reflect his Christian and family roots whilst recognising his uniqueness and individuality. Don't forget to also check out what the initials spell out and how he might feel at school as he grows up with the name you select.

Baptism is a very
special and
sacred moment

Q My mother is keen that our baby should be baptised but my husband says he's not bothered and is happy to leave it to me. Does baptism make any difference today?

A As you'll see from the sacred traditions of baptism on pages 10-11, there are understandable reasons for your mother's attitude — in her view it's simply what's best for your baby, her grandchild.

Baptism is a very special and sacred moment; it's a sign, too, which points to something more complex and lifelong than just the moments of the ceremony. But the promise is only complete as your child grows up. Your own faith carries your child through those days until he can recognise the Christian faith for himself. Clearly, then, if there's no living faith in your home, what takes place at your baby's baptism remains unfulfilled and incomplete.

You may want to think things through in terms of your own approach before making a final decision about a baptism.

Q I heard that you could have different baby naming ceremonies these days. Do I have a choice in the church?

A There are a variety of commercial baby naming services now available outside of the Church and many of them are well constructed and can be personalised for a private occasion. If you're looking for a naming ceremony to recognise and celebrate the arrival of your baby then one of these 'off the peg' customised services may be what you are looking for but it will not be a Baptism. A Baptism is a completely different community event which welcomes your baby into the Christian community.

Q We'd like to get our baby baptised but I'm not keen on having to sign up for preparation sessions. Are they compulsory?

A The purpose of baptism preparation is not to check up on the merits of the parents. It's to reassure you that the Church takes your baby and your family very seriously. The Church wants your baby's baptism to be all that you hope for.

You'll have received plenty of help and advice about all the practical elements of parenting and, if you're lucky, you'll have people around you to provide support and help when needed. The Christian family, the Church, wants to walk beside you and your child as they grow up; in particular, as you bring your child to a maturity of soul and spirit in the light of the gospel of Jesus Christ. That can be a daunting undertaking. The purpose of baptism preparation is to provide an opportunity for you to voice any concerns or doubts you may have about your own role and to inspire you in the days ahead.

Q In the eyes of the Church, what happens to my little girl if she isn't baptised?

A Your little girl is loved fully and completely by God and has been since the moment she was conceived. Baptism doesn't make God love or bless your child any more than before. What baptism offers is the opportunity of a fullness of life, a more complete awareness of the Spirit of God and the richness which that offers in understanding the purpose of life. It could be described as the difference between seeing life in black and white or in full colour.

In the past there was a belief that to be unbaptised was to be somehow 'outside' the fullness of heaven after death. The anxiety to have babies baptised as soon as possible after birth was a sign of the times when infant mortality was a familiar event.

Q When my sister's little boy was baptised the service was held with five other families. Is it possible to have a private ceremony for our baby's baptism?

A No Baptism can be a private event. Your child is being welcomed into the Christian community. An important part of the celebration of baptism is the public recognition of your child and of the community's commitment to you and your family in terms of support, prayers and encouragement. There are also practical reasons in most parishes which restrict individual ceremonies.

A baptism celebration can be a wonderfully rich occasion in a parish. Where there are several families involved, it can also mean a sharing of responsibilities for the ceremony, which can be a relief for some.

# A baptism celebration can be a wonderfully rich occasion in a parish

**Q** I have a little girl from an earlier relationship. Can she be baptised at the same time as my new daughter?

**A** There's no reason why you shouldn't celebrate the two baptisms at one family occasion but you'll need to consider the following points. Every baptism is a unique and one-off occasion simply because each child is unique and individual. This means that you'd be celebrating two separate baptisms not a joint event.

You don't say how old your eldest daughter is. Is she old enough to be included, even in a simple way, in any discussion or decision about her own baptism? Will she need to have the chance to be given an introduction to Christianity and what it offers her? Do you need to consider her birth father's opinion? A member of your baptism team will be able to help with the appropriate preparation required. Only by considering these two baptisms separately can you ensure that you make the right decision for the right reasons.

**Q** I'm not a Christian but my partner is, and she's very keen to have our baby baptised. I don't mind if it makes her happy. What do I have to do?

**A** It's vital to talk about this together. In baptism you're laying down the roots of a Christian family life for your child. This doesn't mean the exclusion of other opinions or approaches but it must be rooted in genuine respect for each other's point of view and values. It's a lovely attitude to say "Whatever makes you happy…" but that can wear thin as the years pass, and nothing can substitute for mutual understanding.

Try to understand why your partner is so keen on baptism for your baby. Try to share your own thoughts on the meaning of life and your understanding of God, perhaps also your personal spirituality. After all, you'll find that you both have to face these kind of questions from your child as she grows up so it's important that you're able to give her an authentic picture of each other's views, reflecting tolerance and understanding.

Baptism preparation can help fill any gaps in understanding or belief for your partner. Sharing the issues raised can help your own discussions together in the days ahead.

**Q** My partner and I aren't married but we'd like to have our little boy baptised. Is that allowed?

**A** Yes, it is. As part of your promises as parents at the baptism you'll be asked to make the solemn promise that you'll accept the responsibility of bringing your child up in the practice of the Catholic faith. The implications of that for you and your partner are something which you'll need to talk about together in order to ensure that you provide a truthful and authentic experience of the promise which you make. Take time to talk this through with your priest and if you want to explore any other areas of concern don't be afraid to do so. The priest, like yourselves, only wants the best for your baby and his future life.

Q A friend at work was received into the Church last Easter; she was baptised at the Vigil. Could a baby have a similar ceremony?

A Traditionally, the Church welcomes new members at the Easter Vigil as this is the key moment of the Church year when the resurrection of Jesus Christ is celebrated. Three days after his crucifixion and death, Jesus rose to eternal life, a life to which we're invited. It's the acceptance of that invitation which we celebrate at baptism.

At one time, all baptisms took place at this time and were conducted by the local bishop. As numbers increased this became impractical but the key elements remain and are present at every baptism. The key elements are outlined on pages 20-21.

# symbols of baptism

## Water

Water brings new life and is also a sign of cleansing. In baptism it represents the flowing waters of the River Jordan where Jesus Christ was himself baptised by John the Baptist and from which he emerged as the chosen one — the beloved Son of God. The water in which your child is baptised will be blessed with the following, or similar, words:

"God of love and mercy, bless this water in which your children are to be reborn. May it cleanse your people and refresh the faith of your Church. We ask this through Christ our Lord."

## Font

In the early days of Christianity, a separate building was often erected near to the church building for the celebration of baptism. This was because baptism is seen as the entrance into the Christian community, the Church.

Usually these special baptistries had a large pool in which the candidates could be totally immersed. Different climates and cultures have modified this practice and large pools aren't often seen any more. These days a font allows the waters of baptism to be poured without total immersion.

Traditionally, a font is placed near the entrance to the church. The added presence of holy water stoups (mini fonts) at the door is a further reminder of our personal entrance to the Christian community through the waters of baptism.

## Oils

The Oils used at your child's baptism will have been blessed by the bishop in the cathedral on Holy Thursday, the day on which the Christian community recalls the Last Supper. These oils are then distributed to the local churches for use throughout the following year.

Oil of Baptism, also known as Oil of Catechumens, is a simple olive oil which is rubbed on the chest as a sign of purification and preparation for the task ahead.

Oil of Chrism is oil which has balm or balsam  added to give a sweet perfume which represents "the aroma of holiness" (2Corinthians 2:15-16). Your child will be anointed with this oil on the crown following baptism. Now a Christian, your child is truly an 'anointed one' for life, with a part to play in the work of Jesus Christ throughout the world. In days to come the promises and profession of faith which you make on behalf of your child at baptism will be confirmed personally by your child at confirmation when Oil of Chrism will be used again.

## Candle

You will be handed a lighted candle on behalf of your child. This candle will have been lit from the large Paschal Candle which was blessed at the Easter Vigil and which represents Jesus Christ, the Light of the world. When the light is passed on to your child by way of the baptismal candle it conveys how the light of Christ will guide your child throughout the rest of their life.

## White garment

Traditionally, in the early Church, baptisms involved total immersion. As the candidates rose out of the water they were wrapped in a white garment which signified the new life in which they had clothed themselves. The giving of a white garment (usually a shawl) to your child reflects exactly the same reality — the new life in the Spirit.

# choosingthe
# scripturereadings

An important element of the first part of your child's baptism ceremony will be listening to the words of Scripture. It's worth taking some time to think about the readings. If you're involved in any group preparation it can help to be familiar with some options. If your child is baptised during the celebration of Mass the readings will be of that Sunday.

Your child's baptism offers you an opportunity to re-visit the Scriptures and reflect upon what it means to follow the call of Christ. Here are a some suggestions you may like to consider.

## GOSPEL READINGS:

**Matthew 22:35-40** Jesus outlines the greatest commandment of all for those who follow him.

**Matthew 28:18-20** The instruction to baptise all peoples.

**Mark 1:9-11** The baptism of Jesus is recalled. This marks the beginning of Jesus' ministry.

**Mark 10:13-16** Jesus welcomes children and instructs his followers to do the same.

**Mark 12:28-34** Jesus teaches the importance of love for God and for one another.

**John 3:1-6** On being born again in the water and in the Spirit.

**John 4:5-14** The symbolism of water as a spring of the living water of eternal life.

**John 6:44-47** Everyone who believes has eternal life.

**John 7:37-39** The fountains of living waters flowing from the Spirit of Christ.

**John 9:1-7** Jesus restores sight to the blind man.

**John 15:1-11** On remaining one with Jesus Christ in order to bear fruit now and eternally.

## OLD TESTAMENT READINGS:

**Exodus 17:3-7** The Lord provides water for his people when their faith wavers in the desert.

**Responsorial Psalm 22** The Lord is my shepherd.

**Ezekiel 36:24-28** The Lord cleanses his people, giving them new heart and new spirit.

**Responsorial Psalm 33** A psalm praising the goodness of God.

## NEW TESTAMENT READINGS:

**Romans 6:3-5** St Paul spells out the nature of baptism.

**1Corinthians 12:12-13** The Spirit unites all who are baptised into one body, the body of Christ today.

**Galatians 3:26-28** All who are baptised are clothed in Christ.

**Ephesians 4:1-6** The importance of unity in one faith and one baptism.

"I baptise you in the name of the Father and of the Son and of the Holy Spirit."

# A Sacred Ceremony

Guiding you through the various stages of your child's baptismal service

# loving: the introduction and the welcome

Your baby is a creation of love. As you present your child for baptism, you may feel overwhelmed by your role as a parent but one thing is certain, you can love your baby into full life through baptism.

The ceremony of baptism begins with a warm greeting to you, your family and friends and most important of all, your baby, along with words of welcome on behalf of the whole Christian Church. The priest will then ask you what name you've chosen for your child saying the following, or similar, words:

"What name have you given your child?"
You reply giving your child's name.
"What do you ask of God's Church for N...?"
You reply, "Baptism".

You'll then be asked to confirm your own intentions and commitment to nurturing this new life of faith within your child. Everyone present is also invited to express to you their support and love in the days ahead.

The words of this greeting are reinforced with the traditional sign of Christianity, the sign of the cross that the minister, parents and godparents trace on the forehead of your child.

This initial greeting expresses the genuine love and commitment which, God has re-assured us, is available to all. In baptism your child is beginning the journey of discovering the richness and the fullness of life.

"Do not stop the children from coming to me, for the kingdom of heaven belongs to such as these." Jesus Christ, Matthew 19:14

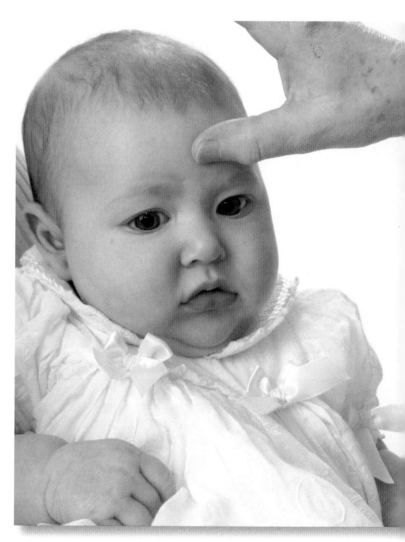

"My dear N..., the Christian community welcomes you with great joy. In its name I claim you for Christ our Saviour by the sign of his cross."

## Anointing with the Oil of Baptism...

Before the waters of baptism are poured over your child, there will be an anointing with the Oil of Baptism. It's also known as the Oil of Catechumens or the Oil of the Saints (see pages 20-21). This anointing on the breast is an act of exorcism (purification) and initiation. It's an anointing of love and promise. Your child is delivered from every evil and assured of the strength and protection of Jesus in the days ahead.

# listening: the words of the Lord...

At this moment in the ceremony, in order to set the scene for the beginning of your child's life of faith, we listen to the word of God read from the New Testament and the Gospel.

These words guide us and reassure us of his love and care for each person present, and for your child. After all, our faith is not simply a spiritual lifestyle plan; it's founded upon the word of God.

The word 'gospel' means 'Good News'. The Good News that Jesus Christ expressed is the certain truth of the resurrection which follows the death of sin and evil. And, that struggle is not between other worldly beings of good and evil but in our day to day life, decision-making and relationships. In the scriptures and in the Gospel especially, Jesus speaks to you personally. Everyone present then adds their words, in the form of prayers for you and your child, your family and friends. We then reach out to the wider family of the Church, and the world, in words of love and mutual concern.

## ...The promises are made

Following the anointing, you and your child's godparents, will be asked to reaffirm your own rejection of evil and your personal trust in God.

## His words guide us and reassure us

# lifting: pouring of the baptismal water...

Water brings life to our world in a million different ways. The baptism of Jesus in the Jordan, is the starting point for our understanding of Christian baptism. The flowing water of the Jordan is replaced by the sacramental use of water, blessed at the Easter Vigil, and through this symbolism, we rise to a new life in Christ. At your child's baptism this blessed water is poured over your child three times in the name of the Trinity, Father, Son and Holy Spirit.

"N… I baptise you in the name of the Father and of the Son and of the Holy Spirit."

Your child is baptised. Your wish for your child to be given life as part of the Christian community has begun.
This is a sacred moment of initiation.

You as parents must now guide your chid to maturity and to the completion of their initiation by Confirmation and Eucharist.

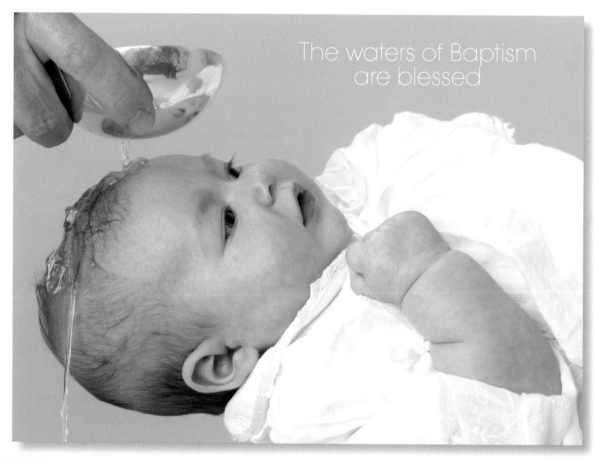

The waters of Baptism are blessed

# ...the symbolic rites

We know from personal experience that baptism does not ensure perfection for life. The personal struggles with right and wrong, selfishness and unselfishness, will continue. Baptism isn't a magic rite and it doesn't guarantee that evil no longer has any power over us. But we can always choose to overcome it if we live in the Spirit of Christ. And so, further symbolic rites express elements of what has taken place:

■ Your child is anointed again, this time on the crown of the head with Oil of Chrism. The name Christ means the Anointed One. Chrism, a sweet smelling oil, is used as a sign that, in union with Christ, your child is the 'Anointed One', called to share in the life, death and resurrection of the Lord.

■ Your child is wrapped in a white garment. It's a sign of the new life in which your child now embraces.

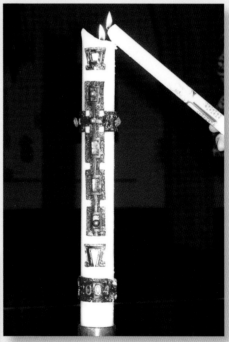

■ Your child is given a candle which has been lit from the Paschal candle. The Paschal Candle symbolises Christ, the Light of the world. Your child too, is called to bring a light to the world through the ways of Jesus Christ.

■ Your child may also be touched on the ears and mouth as a sign that he or she will only hear and speak what is creative and life-giving in reflection of the life of Christ.

# living:

## reciting the Lord's Prayer

Together everyone present joins in the family prayer of Christians, the Lord's Prayer. This prayer is the foundation for life following our baptism into the Church:

### "Our Father, who art in heaven, hallowed be thy name."

God is our heavenly parent, totally committed to each of us and to our well-being. The recognition of God's love leads us to worship and praise the Lord and also to try to live the gospel each day.

### "Thy kingdom come. Thy will be done on earth, as it is in heaven."

Jesus Christ came to show us the reality of the kingdom of God. His words in the Gospels and in those parables which he uses to illustrate the kingdom of God, are a map for each of us to follow.

### "Give us this day our daily bread."

We ask for all that we need to be fully alive in mind, body and spirit. And in praying this line we acknowledge our responsibility to care for others as the hands and feet of Christ today.

### "And forgive us our trespasses, as we forgive those who trespass against us."

This is the toughest part of our family prayer: a trade off with God that we will experience forgiveness at the level we have expressed to others. We need God's help to do this.

### "And lead us not into temptation, but deliver us from evil."

There is a great power within all of us which we can use for good or evil. With God's help, through prayer, we can use this power for good.

## We're safe in the arms of the one who loves us most of all

We are safe, we can relax, we remind ourselves that it is God's world, God's creation. Just as nothing comes between your child and God at this moment, we too, are safe in the arms of the one who loves each of us most of all.

This family prayer will be followed by special prayers for you, your child and for each person who has joined in the celebration of the baptism of your child.

# order of service

**The baptism service is in four parts:**

**1.** The welcome of ........................takes place at the door of the Church.

**2.** The word (which is nourishment for the Journey is read at the lectern or ambo.

**3.** The sacramental action takes place at the font

**4.** The conclusion – which includes the Our Father gathers us around the altar where, when our child is older he/she will receive the Eucharist.

Welcome and naming

Reading from Scripture

The Baptism

of

Prayer of Intercession and the invocation of the Saints.

Baptismal Promises made by the parents and godparents

on behalf of the child

The Baptism: the pouring of the waters of baptism

Anointing with the Oil of Chrism

Enrobing in the white garment of grace

Reception of the Light of Christ for the days ahead

# finding strength in prayer

Once the ceremony is over, the work of living a life of love continues for each of us in very different ways. Try to remember those who joined in your child's baptism in your prayers. The unity which the ceremony expresses is a reality. It's a true bond between all present, not just during the event but permanently.

We're called to transfigure the world with kindness, generosity, healing and tolerance. The words of Jesus Christ will guide us. Share them with your child in the years ahead.

## Discovering your map of life

Sometimes it's said that nobody gets a map of life anymore. Unlike past times we seem to have no certainty of destination and family relationships are fluid. The lack of a map in life, as on the ground, can lead to a loss of direction, lack of confidence and weariness.

True prayer helps to root us in the life of the one Person who offers direction. As Jesus himself said it, offers 'rest for your souls' (Matthew 11:30). But prayer is a waste of time if it makes no difference.

One of the best images of a good life is given to us by St Francis de Sales. He suggests that our life should be like a small child walking along a country road with his or her parent: as they walk together the child is picking the blackberries with one hand whilst the other holds the parent's hand tightly. Every so often the child looks up at the parent — just to check that everything is OK.

This image is a great description of our daily life: on the one hand we concentrate on the concerns of the day — family, work, making the most of the world in which we live and enjoying its fruits; on the other hand, we keep a prayerful eye on our loving God. Why not renew your own prayer life at this special time.

## What can prayer bring to our lives

■ Prayer gives us a deeper sense of self-worth and helps us to appreciate that we are precious to God. Christianity is not a religion, it is a relationship; and prayer is the life-blood of that relationship. It's being with the God who makes us and loves us. In prayer we come to know God as "…Daddy".

■ Prayer makes us more grateful. It helps us to appreciate what we have and so encourages us to share what we have with others. Some people are good at 'giving out' at the wrongs in our world but do nothing about them. A grateful person 'gives out' of himself or herself and realises that "for things to change, I have to change".

■ Closely linked with gratitude is praise. When we can find it in ourself to offer praise we become more like the person we praise. Many of us forget or fail to praise and remain in misery. True praise takes us out of ourself and our limited world into the kingdom of heaven.

■ Our gratitude and praise leads us to worship. True prayer leads to true worship with others. For Catholics this means prayer, where possible, in the household and, above all, in the Eucharist, in which we celebrate our communion with God and our commitment to each other. "Where two or three meet in my name, I shall be there with them," (Matthew 18:20) says Jesus, reminding us that prayer brings us closer, not only to God, but to one another.

Prayer helps us to appreciate that we're precious to God

## Try a little meditation...

Take a prayer or scripture passage. This can be a prayer that you like, the Lord's Prayer or a passage from scripture — anything that gives some insight into God's ways or which strikes a chord with you. Turn the passage over in your heart and mind. Do this by taking the points from the passage that particularly strike you. Trust your own thoughts and be yourself. If you don't understand something, say this to God. If you feel irritated by something tell this to God.

It's important to recognise that, when Jesus spoke, he didn't expect to be understood immediately: the parables, for example, were an invitation to think about and to puzzle over what he was saying so that the point, when it does occur to us, 'strikes home'. The "asking" that Jesus referred to is the foundation of prayer: "Ask, and it will be given to you... For the one who asks always receives..." (Matthew 7:7)

# living the dream

Most of us have dreamt about what kind of a parent we'll be. Reflecting upon our own childhood and on the person we've become, we can be pretty clear about our future family life. But it's easy to lose that dream in the worries and workload of day to day family life. What steps can you take to make that dream a reality; a force for a creative and fulfilling family life?

When you become a parent your life is changed — forever. How can you manage that change? How do you ensure that you don't lose your dream, your vision and values of parenting? The answer is to take some time to put some flesh on the bones of your dream at this stage.

■ What key values do you consider to be of paramount importance?
■ How will you endeavour to instill these values in your child?
■ What kind of culture do you want to create in your family and in your home?
■ What customs and traditions would you like to introduce or retain from your own and your partner's upbringing?
■ How will you deal with anger, betrayal or disappointment?

Once you've had a chance to think through and discuss these questions write down five or six clear statements which illustrate the key points that you've identified as important. Write each of these statements on a separate page.

For example: "In our family we show respect to every person at all times."

Follow your statement with a description of what it's like when this happens within your family. How does it feel? How do you act in controversial situations? What kind of words are used?

Think about whether you can stick by your statement and ensure this happens purely as a result of your own efforts or whether you'll need the help and/or co-operation of others. If the latter is the case, how will you do this?

Think too, about which elements of your statement are beyond your control. What is there about it that you'll be unable to influence either alone or with others? How could you handle that?

Once you've completed each page, make a decision on whether you really want to move forward on this lifestyle change and if so, write in a date on which you'll begin to live by your own personal dream.

when you become a parent your life is changed - forever

By asking for baptism for your child, even if you don't think of yourself as very religious, you're recognising that God is part of your life and of your decision making. Some of your other reasons for wanting to celebrate your child's baptism are probably that you'd like a public naming and recognition of your child and an opportunity to celebrate the birth with your family and friends — all excellent reasons and natural reactions to becoming a parent.

All of these aspects are also key points of good parenting:

■ An openness to living creatively in partnership with God
■ Recognition and respect for one another
■ A celebration of life and its gifts

**Redemptorist Communications**
Liguori House
75 Orwell Road
Rathgar
Dublin 6

00353 (0) 1492 2488
www.redcoms.org
email: sales@redcoms.org

Let's Celebrate a Baptism

© Rosemary Gallagher

ISBN 978-0-9558906-0-4

Second printing: January 2009

Imprimatur: **Diarmuid Martin, Archbishop of Dublin**
The Imprimatur is a declaration that a book or pamphlet is considered to be free from doctrinal or moral error. It is not implied that those who have granted the Imprimatur agree with the contents, opinions and statements expressed.

Design: **Attica Design**

Photography: **Cox Photography and iStockphoto**

Printed by: **Graham and Heslip Ltd, Belfast.**

This book is printed on paper which contains wood from well-managed forests, certified in accordance with the rules of the Forest Stewardship Council.